SCHOLASTIC SCIENCE READERS™

LEVEL
1
AGES 5 AND 6

W9-AWS-754

HUMAN BODY

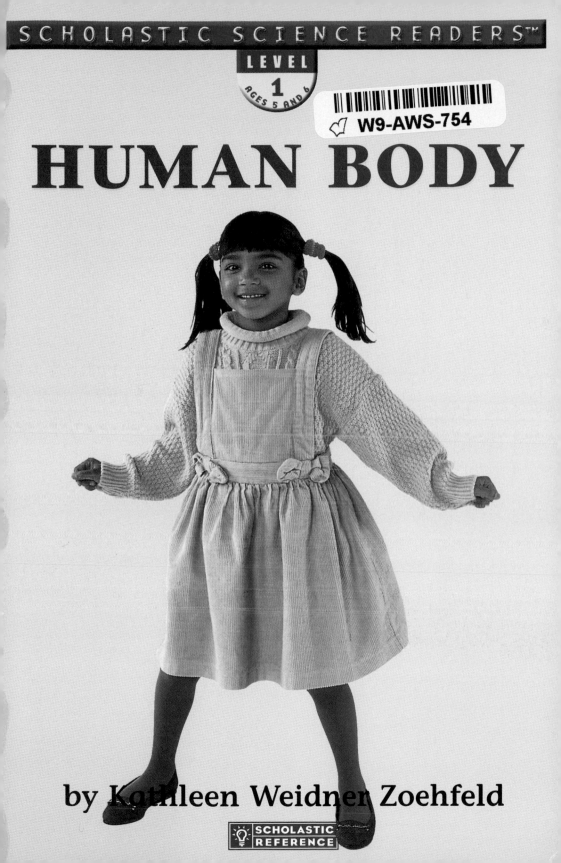

by Kathleen Weidner Zoehfeld

SCHOLASTIC
REFERENCE

PHOTO CREDITS: Cover: Elie Bernager/Tony Stone Images. Page 1: Nancy Sheehan/PhotoEdit; 3: Richard Hutchings/PhotoEdit; 4: Richard Hutchings/PhotoEdit; 5: Myrleen Ferguson Cate/PhotoEdit; 6: Myrleen Ferguson Cate/PhotoEdit; 7: David Young-Wolff/PhotoEdit; 9: Myrleen Ferguson Cate/PhotoEdit; 10, top: Tony Freeman/PhotoEdit; 10, bottom: David Young-Wolff/ PhotoEdit; 11: Richard Hutchings/PhotoEdit; 12: Tom McCarthy/PhotoEdit; 13: Michael Newman/PhotoEdit; 14: Barbara Stitzer/PhotoEdit; 15: Myrleen Ferguson Cate/PhotoEdit; 16: Bill Aron/PhotoEdit; 18: Richard Hutchings/PhotoEdit; 19: David Young-Wolff/PhotoEdit; 21: David Young-Wolff/PhotoEdit; 22-23: Myrleen Ferguson Cate/PhotoEdit; 24: Richard Hutchings/PhotoEdit; 26: Tony Freeman/PhotoEdit; 27: Nancy Shehan/PhotoEdit; 28: David Young-Wolff/PhotoEdit; 29: Kathy Ferguson/PhotoEdit; 30: Tony Freeman/PhotoEdit.

ISBN 0-439-16296-3

Book design by Barbara Balch and Kay Petronio

20 19 18 17 16 15 14 13 12 11 10 09 08   05 06 07 08 09

Printed in the U.S.A.   23

First printing, September 2000

We are grateful to Francie Alexander, reading specialist, and to
Adele M. Brodkin, Ph.D., developmental psychologist, for their
contributions to the development of this series.

Our thanks also to our science consultant Dr. Roland Shook,
professor of natural sciences at Western New Mexico University.

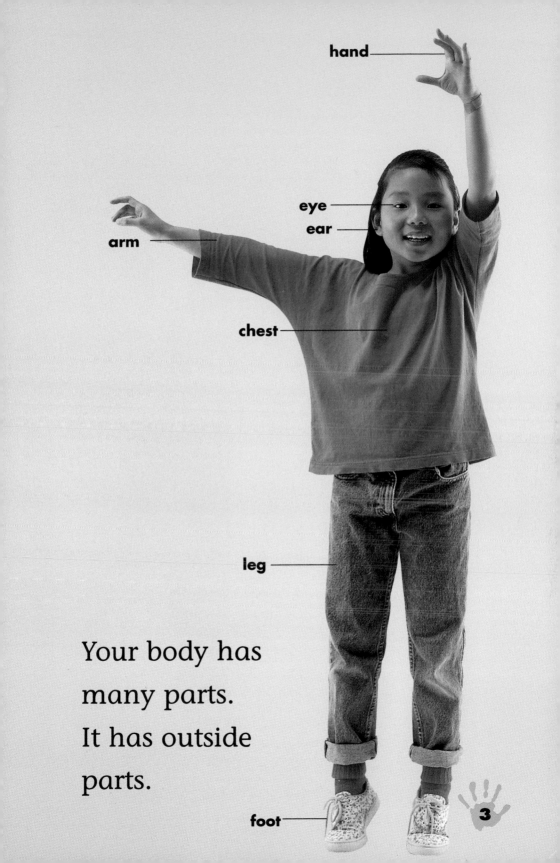

hand

eye

ear

arm

chest

leg

Your body has
many parts.
It has outside
parts.

foot

3

brain

bone

heart

stomach

muscle

And it has
inside parts.

4

Most of your body is covered
by skin.

Your skin helps you feel if something is cold or hot, soft or hard, smooth or rough.

When you touch a kitten,
a message goes from your skin
to your brain.

Your brain understands the message. Your brain tells you the kitten is soft.

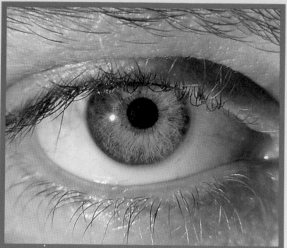

eye

Different parts of your body
send messages to your brain.

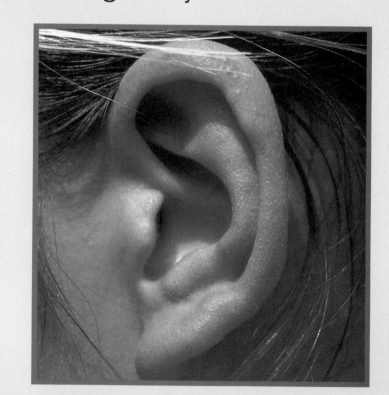

ear

Your brain
helps you
understand
them all.

hand

Your eyes send messages
to your brain. Your brain tells
you the shapes and colors of
the things you see.

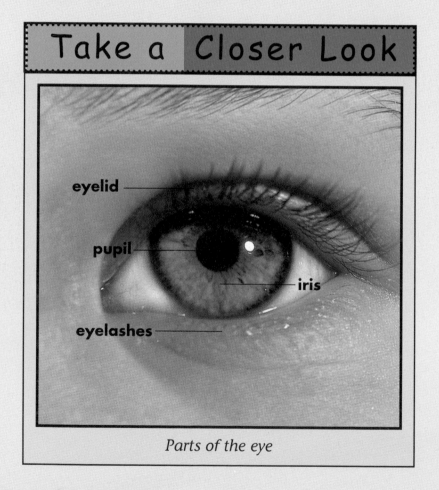

Take a Closer Look

eyelid

pupil

iris

eyelashes

Parts of the eye

Your ears send messages.
Your brain helps you understand
all the sounds you hear.

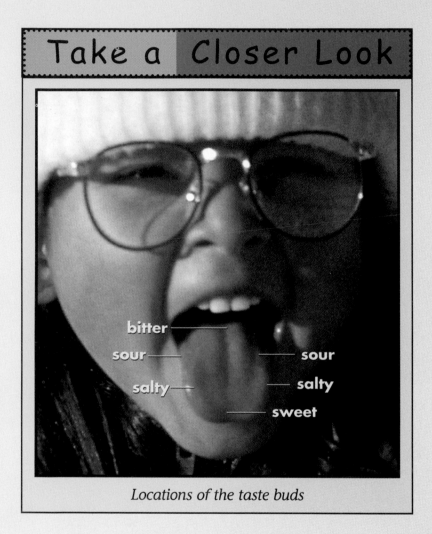

Locations of the taste buds

The **taste buds** on your tongue send messages about the food you eat.

Your brain tells you if your food is salty, sour, bitter, or sweet.

Your nose sends messages to your brain. Your brain can tell if something smells good or bad.

When your brain gets messages from your five **senses**, it tells your body what to do.

Your brain sends messages
to your muscles (**muhss**-uhlz).
Those messages tell your
muscles how to move.

Muscles and bones help you
run, walk, lift, and bend.

Muscles pull on bones in your legs and arms, and in other parts of your body.

*One of the muscles in your arm is called the biceps (**bye**-seps).*

For all that muscle power, you need a lot of **energy**. And the best way to get energy is to eat!

When you swallow a bite of food, it moves down your food tube into your stomach.

Special juices in your stomach **digest** the food.

Then your body can take in
simple things such as **sugars**
from the food. Sugars give you
energy.

To use the energy
from those sugars,
your body also needs
oxygen (**ok**-suh-juhn).
When you breathe,
your lungs take in
oxygen from the air.

The oxygen goes into your blood. Sugars from your food go into your blood, too.

Take a Closer Look

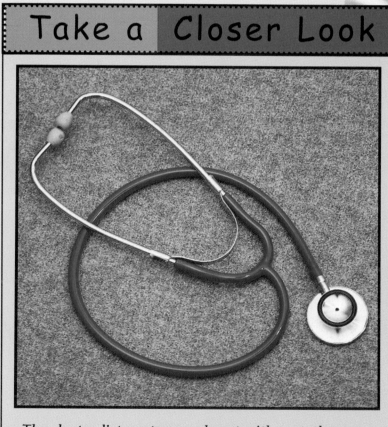

*The doctor listens to your heart with a stethoscope (**steth**-uh-skope).*

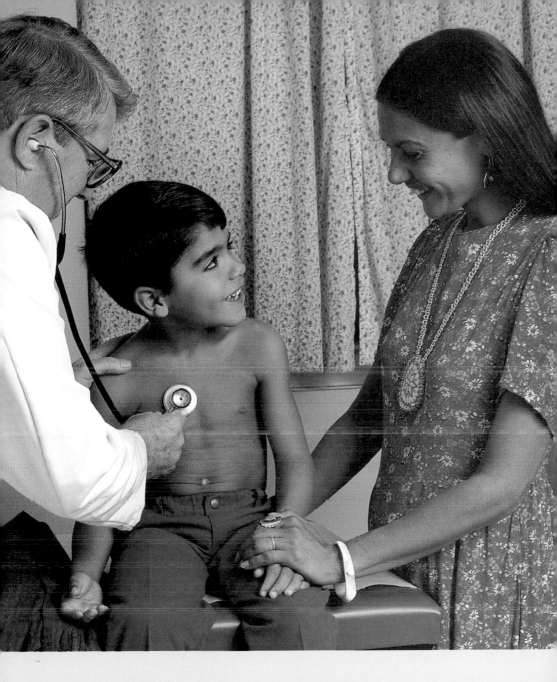

Your heart pumps blood to
all the parts of your body.

This gives you the energy
to run, talk, laugh, and grow.

Even when you are asleep, your heart keeps pumping. You keep on breathing.

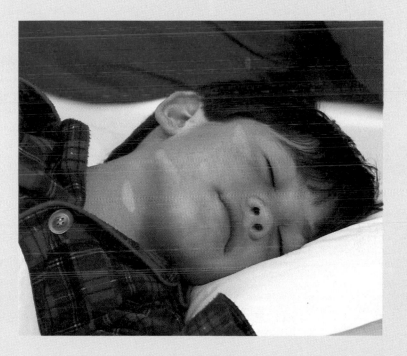

And your brain makes sure
ALL your body parts are working
just right.

Glossary

digest—to break food down into simpler parts that can be taken in and used by the body for energy and for growing

energy—the ability or power to do work

oxygen (**ok**-suh-juhn)—one of the main gases in the air

senses—the ways that we become aware of the things around us

sugars—a simple, sweet part of most foods. Sugars can give energy to the body.

taste buds—tiny, round bunches of cells found on the top of the tongue that help us taste our food

A Note to Parents

Learning to read is such an exciting time in a child's life. You may delight in sharing your favorite fairy tales and picture books with your child.

But don't forget the importance of introducing your child to the world of nonfiction. The ability to read and comprehend factual material will be essential to your child in school, and throughout life. The Scholastic Science Readers™ series was created especially with beginning readers in mind. These books, with their clear texts and beautiful photographs, will help you to share the wonders of science with *your* new reader.

Suggested Activity

Here's an easy way to help your child understand the concept of body parts that are either inside, or outside. Start by having him or her lie down on a large sheet of paper. Trace the outline of your child's body. Then help him or her to label all the familiar outside parts.

Next, have your child draw in and label the inside parts of the body. Things needn't get too technical: a simple heart and brain will do, along with basic bones, muscles, and blood vessels. This will reinforce your child's understanding of the body parts that can't be seen, where they are, and what they do.